AMERICAN BLACK HISTORY
Reference Manual

By Ted Terry

Y0-CBB-577

MYLES PUBLISHING
Tulsa, Oklahoma

Reference Handbook on
American Black History

© 1991 by Ted Terry

Manufactured in the United States.
First Edition.

Myles Publishing
Tulsa, Oklahoma

ISBN 0-9625498-0-0

© Myles Publishing

DEDICATION

John Lamar Hill, Sr.

This book is dedicated to a great community leader and longtime friend.

I thank him for being a true role model and for giving me the opportunity to grow.

Thanks, John

CONTENTS

ACKNOWLEDGMENTS

Praise and thanks to my God for the many blessings he has given to me. And also for allowing me to stay the course.

Thanks to my mother, who really believes in me.

To my son, Torrance, and my daughter, Tracie. I love you dearly.

To all of you who have shared in my life, the good and the bad.

Thanks to Larry Harris for a fine book cover; Casey and her family; Aunt Etha Lee for her help and Jackie Terry and Joan Jones.

Thanks to Sam Harris, Susan Coman & Associates, Dr. Charles Lewis, Howard University, T. Oscar Chapelle, Sammeerah Muhammad, Hazel Bibb, Leona Young, Juanita Moore, and Jeryl Busby, President of Motown Records.

INTRODUCTION

*"We ask for nothing that we can do our-
selves, nothing has been bought that
Black people cannot produce. There is no
short cut to achievement, life requires
thorough preparation."*

GEORGE WASHINGTON CARVER

The fact that Black people in the United States have made substantial progress is amply shown to be true by the many universities, colleges, and schools supported and manned by the Black race. However, the contributions of Afro-Americans in helping to shape America through discovery, pioneering, and development of ideas has not been adequately presented in textbooks, mass media, and other communication from written records about America. This book is designed to present some important facts about the contributions of Black Americans.

From the cradle of civilization we came; some from the west, some from the east and some from the north. A civilization that existed long before the western world.

Africa is our homeland, a land that is rich and fertile, a land where Egypt was an especially attractive land, warm in climate and eminently suited for human beings who had not yet learned how to live with ease in colder areas. The Nile ran past Egypt's doorstep. Our ancestors built the pyramids "high above the Nile".

Civilization existed in Ghana, Melle, Songhey. There, Kings and Queens ruled with discipline.

Gao, Walata, Timbuktu, and Jenne, became intellectual centers at which were concentrated the most learned scholars of West Africa, where most of the slaves were captured, and to which scholars from Asia and Europe came for consultation and study. Here our ancestors studied medicine, astronomy and mathematics.

The African way of life held a cultural heritage that is richly surrounded by the family. And among many of our people there was knowledge of basketry, textile weaving, pottery and woodwork. We developed the art of manufacturing and using iron. In Benin, we used bronze and copper; in Melle, we used silver and gold.

We traded with other civilizations long before Columbus discovered America.

We gave the world great carvings and sculptures of wood, stone, ivory, bronze, brass, glass and clay, thus giving witness to the artwork of our homeland, Africa!

Africa is music and music is Africa. We gave the world the xylophone, the violin, guitar, zither, harp, flute and drums. And, of course, the song, with or without instrumental accompaniment.

We introduced storytelling to the world through our handing down the oral traditions, moral tales, supernatural tales, proverbs, epic poems, satire, love songs, funeral pieces and comic tales. Our Groits sang, told stories and recited poetry. They kept in their memories the history, laws and traditions of our people and were themselves living dictionaries.

Such was the way of life in our homeland – Africa! At the end of the sixteenth century, Europeans began to make way for the trading in men. The trading was known as the slave trade. History tells us that five, ten, fifteen millions were brought from the shores of Africa, some to be settled in the Caribbean, Cuba, Puerto Rico, Jamaica, Spain, Brazil and on to America.

Many took to the sea and preferred death to the life that awaited them in America.

In America, the slaves were to remain slaves until death. In America, they were treated like animals, sold from their families, denied education, denied full citizenship.

From the pages of history comes the images of African American History. Images of great men and women who struggled to be free, who were descendents of Africa.

Q. What novelist wrote *Uncle Tom's Children*?

A. *Richard Wright*

·

Q. Lorraine Hansberry wrote what Broadway hit?

A. *Raisin in the Sun*

·

Q. The *Red Book* is the first authenticated record of lynchings. Can you name the author?

A. *Ida B. Wells*

·

Q. Born in Oklahoma City, Oklahoma, this Black novelist wrote the novel *The Invisible Man,* for which he won the national Book Award for fiction in 1952.

A. *Ralph Waldo Ellison*

·

Q. Who wrote a number one best seller depicting fact and fiction of the history of his family, beginning in Africa in the mid-1700s, which later became a 12-hour series for television?

A. *Alex Haley*

Q. Who wrote the book *Uncle Tom's Cabin*, which characterized the plight of the slaves?

A. *Harriet Beecher Stowe*

Q. What is Nat Love noted for?

A. *Wrote the first western story*

Q. How many books did Martin Luther King write?

A. *Five*

Q. Who is Paul Laurence Dunbar and where was he born?

A. *Renowned poet, born in Dayton, Ohio*

Q. Who wrote *From Slavery to Freedom*, a detailed volume on the history of Black Americans?

A. *John Hope Franklin*

Q. Who is the author of the biography of Martin Luther King, Jr., *What Manner of Man*?

A. *Lerone Bennett, Jr.*

Q. What Black historian wrote a history book called *The Black Abolitionists*?

A. *Benjamin Quarles*

Q. Name the well-known poet who wrote *A Negro Love Song*.

A. *Paul Laurence Dunbar*

Q. Name the man who authored the book *Born to Rebel* in 1971.

A. *Benjamin E. Mays*

Q. *The Color Purple* is the Pulitzer Prize winning novel of what noted writer?

A. *Alice Walker*

•

Q. What famous Black American wrote the classic children's book *The Lost Zoo*?

A. *Countee Cullen*

•

Q. Who is the author of *Blues People*?

A. *Imamu Amiri Baraka / aka Leroi Jones*

•

Q. What is the book *Blues People* about?

A. *Negro music in America*

•

Q. Name the Black woman who was commended by President George Washington for her literary skill.

A. *Phillis Wheatley*

•

Q. Langston Hughes is known best for what?

A. *His poetry*

•

Q. Who wrote *American Negro Slave Revolts*?

A. *Herbert Aptheker, 1943*

Q. Who wrote *Before the Mayflower*?

A. *Lerone Bennett, Jr., 1969*

Q. Who wrote *Chronological History of the Negro in America*?

A. *Peter M. Bergman, 1968*

Q. Who wrote *Black Metropolis*?

A. *Horace Clayton, 1945*

Q. Who wrote *The African Origin of Civilization*?

A. *Anta Cheikh Diop, 1969*

Q. Who wrote *The Negro Freedman*?

A. *Donald H. Henderson, 1952*

Q. Who wrote *A History of the African People*, 2nd Edition?

A. *Robert W. July, 1974*

Q. Who wrote *The Negro in the Making of America*?

A. *Benjamin Quarles, 1964*

·

Q. Who wrote *American Negro in the World War*?

A. *Emmett J. Scott, 1919*

·

Q. Who wrote *They Came Before Columbus*?

A. *Ivan Van Sertima, 1976*

·

Q. Who wrote *The Destruction of Black Civilization*?

A. *Chancellor Williams, 1974*

·

AWARDS

Q. Dr. Ralph Bunche was the first Black American to win what award?

A. *Nobel Peace Prize, in 1950*

Q. Name this great musician to whom President Richard Nixon presented the Presidential Medal of Freedom in 1969.

A. *Duke Ellington*

Q. Who was the youngest man to receive the Nobel Peace Prize, at age 35?

A. *Martin Luther King, Jr.*

Q. Who was the first Black to win the Pulitzer Prize for her book of poetry?

A. *Gwendolyn Brooks*

Q. What was the name of the book written by Gwendolyn Brooks and when was it published?

A. *Annie Allen, 1949*

Q. What ragtime piano player/musician was awarded the Pulitzer Prize after his death?

A. *Scott Joplin*

Q. In 1963, President Lyndon B. Johnson presented the Medal of Freedom to this great opera singer. Who was she?

A. *Marian Anderson*

Q. Who was the first Black to be inducted into the Hall of Fame of Great Americans?

A. *Booker T. Washington*

Q. In what war did William H. Carney receive the Congressional Medal of Honor?

A. *The Spanish American War*

Q. Who was the first Black man to receive the Congressional Medal of Honor since the Spanish American War?

A. *PFC William Thompson*

Q. Who was the first Black to win the NAACP Springarn Medal?

A. *Biologist Ernest E. Just*

Q. Who was awarded the Nobel Peace Prize for his opposition to the apartheid policy in South Africa?

A. *Anglican Bishop Desmond Tutu*

Q. Vanessa Williams was crowned Miss America for 1984, becoming the first Black to win in how many years of the pageant's history?

A. *62 years*

Q. From which war did PFC William Thompson receive his Congressional Medal of Honor?

A. *Korean War*

Q. Who was the first Black to receive the Congressional Medal of Honor?

A. *William H. Carney*

Q. Who was the second black Miss America?

A. *Suzette Charles*

■

Q. Who was the second Black named to the Hall of Fame of Great Americans?

A. *George Washington Carver*

■

Q. Who was the first Black American to receive the CPAE (National Speaker Council of Peers Award of Excellence)?

A. *Les Brown*

■

CIVIL RIGHTS

Q. What Mississippi NAACP civil rights leader was slain in 1963?

A. *Medgar Evers*

■

Q. What national Black organization was founded on President Abraham Lincoln's birthday?

A. *NAACP (National Association for the Advancement of Colored People)*

■

Q. Who signed the Emancipation Proclamation?

A. *President Abraham Lincoln*

■

Q. Name the ordained Baptist minister who was unanimously elected executive director of the NAACP in 1977.

A. *Benjamin L. Hooks*

■

Q. Yolanda, Martin III, Dexter, and Denise are children of what great civil rights leader?

A. *Martin Luther King, Jr.*

■

Q. What is the oldest civil rights organization in America?

A. *NAACP*

Q. What president signed the Civil Rights Bill on April 11, 1968?

A. *President Lyndon B. Johnson*

Q. In what year was the historic March on Washington?

A. *1963*

Q. In the 1960s, what became the weapon for nonviolent protests?

A. *The sit-in*

Q. President John F. Kennedy was in office when this nonviolent Civil Rights weapon was used. Name it.

A. *Sit-in*

Q. The 1908 Springfield, Illinois Race Riot sparked the formation of what?

A. *NAACP*

Q. "Burn, baby, burn" was the phrase that came out of this riot in the 1960s. What Los Angeles section had this riot?

A. *Watts*

Q. In what state was the first Jim Crow Law enacted?

A. *Mississippi*

Q. Why was the Jim Crow Law enacted?

A. *To enforce discrimination against the Negroes by legal enforcement or traditional sanctions.*

Q. What Black educator renounced his American citizenship to become a citizen of Ghana?

A. *William E.B. Du Bois*

Q. Who did Robert Russa Moton succeed as President of Tuskegee Institute?

A. *Booker T. Washington*

Q. What is the largest Black university in the United States?

A. *Howard University*

Q. What agricultural genius was the first Black student to be admitted to Simpson College in Indianola, Iowa?

A. *George Washington Carver*

Q. Over 40 Black colleges benefit from this fund. Can you name it?

A. *UNCF/United Negro College Fund*

Q. What man was the most influential Black educator of his time in America? He was the founder and President of Tuskegee Institute. He was born a slave in 1856.

A. *Booker T. Washington*

Q. What college was established in Texas in 1881 by poor illiterate exslaves and Baptist missionaries?

A. *Bishop College*

Q. Who gained national recognition for her success in teaching unwanted ghetto children in Chicago?

A. *Marva Collins*

Q. What Black educator had only $1.50 to start a school that today bears her name?

A. *Mary McCleod Bethune Cookman College*

Q. Talladega College is in what state?

A. *Alabama*

Q. What is Famous Amos' real name?

A. *Wally Amos*

•

Q. Who was the first Black to be admitted to the University of Mississippi?

A. *James Meredith*

•

Q. Who was the first Black student to graduate from the University of Alabama?

A. *Vivian Malone*

•

Q. George Washington Carver was called the Negro "Wizard of Agriculture" for his research in chemistry. From what university did he graduate?

A. *Iowa State University*

•

Q. Who was the first Black woman president of Wilberforce University?

A. *Yvonne Taylor*

•

Q. Who was the first Black to be admitted to the University of Boston Law School?

A. *Barbara Jordan*

■

Q. Who was the first Black to receive a Ph.D. from Harvard University?

A. *W. E. B. Du Bois*

■

Q. Who was the first Black to become President of Howard University?

A. *Mordecai W. Johnson*

■

Q. Charlotte Ray was the first Black woman to graduate from what prestigious university law school in the 1800s?

A. *Howard University*

■

Q. Name the organization that Dr. Frederick Patterson founded.

A. *United Negro College Fund*

■

Q. Educator John Hope Franklin was appointed chairman of what college's history department in 1956?

A. *Brooklyn College*

•

Q. Who is the founder of Lincoln University?

A. *James Turner*

•

Q. In 1915, this Black American organized the Association for the Study of Negro Life and History. In 1916 he established the *Journal of Negro History*. Who is he?

A. *Dr. Carter G. Woodson*

•

Q. What college was named after Martin Luther King, Jr. and Malcolm X?

A. *Malcolm-King College*

•

Q. What ex-slave received an honorary degree from Harvard University, along with Alexander Graham Bell?

A. *Booker T. Washington*

•

Q. Name two of the three states with the largest Black population.

A. *New York, Texas, and California*

■

Q. In 1905, he launched a movement that consisted of Black intellectuals and professionals: The Niagra Movement. Name him.

A. *W. E. B. Du Bois*

■

Q. Former President of the United Negro College Fund, in 1972 he became the chief executive officer of the National Urban League.

A. *Vernon Jordan, Jr.*

■

Q. What is the name of the oldest Black insurance firm, which was founded in 1893?

A. *Southern Aid Life Insurance Company*

■

Q. Name the speech in which Booker T. Washington urged Blacks to accept segregation in exchange for economics.

A. *The Atlanta Compromise*

■

Q. Before he changed his name, what was Martin Luther King, Jr. known as?

A. *Michael Luther King*

•

Q. Malcolm X was assassinated in what year?

A. *1964 (February)*

•

Q. The European slave trade began in what year?

A. *1441*

•

Q. What term was first used in Great Britain to express strong views against the Atlantic slave trade?

A. *Abolition*

•

Q. What was used by the Portuguese to justify slave trading in the 1400s?

A. *Christianity*

•

Q. The invention of the cotton gin by inventor Eli Whitney brought about a greater need for what type of labor?

A. *Slave labor*

Q. The American Anti-Slavery Society was founded in what year?

A. *1831*

Q. In 1856, a government ruling was handed down saying that Negroes were not human. What federal judicial branch handed down the decision?

A. *United States Supreme Court*

Q. At what age was Martin Luther King, Jr. killed?

A. *Thirty-nine*

Q. Thousands attended the funeral of The Rev. Dr. Martin Luther King, Jr. At what church were memorial services held for him?

A. *Ebenezer Baptist Church*

Q. Chief Sam, Pop Singleton, William Ellis, Paul Cuffee, Major Martin Delany, Dr. Thorne, and Marcus Garvey were well known for what movement?

A. *Back to Africa Movement (The Transatlantic Society)*

•

Q. From 1861 to what year did Negro soldiers fight in the Union army?

A. *1865*

•

Q. Phillip Reed, a slave, fitted and placed this structure atop the United States Capitol Building in Washington, D.C. Can you name the structure?

A. *Statue of Freedom*

•

Q. What was the slave voyage to the Americas known as?

A. *The Middle Passage*

•

Q. During the voyage to the Americas, what ceremony was held by the slave traders to avoid depression?

A. *The Dance of the Slaves*

■

Q. What two battles during the American Revolution were Blacks most instrumental in?

A. *The battles of Bunker Hill & Lexington*

■

Q. What is the name of the Harlem club where many legendary Black entertainers got their start?

A. *The Cotton Club*

■

Q. Homer Adolph Plessy, the man arrested for entering a railroad, took the case to the Supreme Court and came away with what decision?

A. *Separate-but-equal decision*

■

Q. The word Carpetbagger originated out of what war?

A. *Civil War*

■

Q. In what year was the Martin Luther King, Jr. holiday signed into law?

A. *1983*

•

Q. What Black astronaut was killed on his second space flight?

A. *Ronald McNair (The Challenger Mission)*

•

Q. J. Ernest Wilkins earned his Ph.D. at the age of seventeen, to become one of the world's leading mathematicians. He was also one of six Black scientists who helped in the making of the first what?

A. *Atomic bomb*

•

Q. What was the war between the states known as?

A. *The Civil War*

•

HISTORY

People

Q. There were four all-Black regiments of cavalry and infantry who fought in the Southwest Indian wars. What were they called?

A. *The Buffalo Soldiers*

■

Q. This legendary explorer founded the city known as Chicago in the 18th century. Who was he?

A. *Jean Baptiste Point Du Sable*

■

Q. This Black patriot was with General George Washington on the famous voyage across the Delaware River. Who was he?

A. *Oliver Cromwell*

■

Q. Who was the first Black man to pilot a space shuttle? (He was also the third Black man in space).

A. *Frederick Gregory*

Q. What word commonly was used to describe an ex-slave after the Civil War?

A. *Freedman*

Q. Before his death in 1983, he was the President of Kenya. Who was he?

A. *Jomo Kenyatta*

Q. During his presidency, he and congress wanted to colonize slaves in the Caribbean country Haiti. Name the President.

A. *President Abraham Lincoln*

Q. Who was the first Black to address the National Press Club?

A. *Martin Luther King, Jr.*

Q. Composer and bandleader, he died in 1975. His name was Edward Kennedy. Who was he really?

A. *Duke Ellington*

■

Q. Who was the slave who led the bloodiest revolt in American history?

A. *Nat Turner*

■

Q. What is Malcolm X's real name?

A. *Malcolm Little*

■

Q. Phoebe Fraunces, the daughter of "Black Sam Fraunces," is credited for saving the life of which great President?

A. *George Washington*

■

Q. Who is considered responsible for Napoleon selling the Louisiana Territory to the United States after the Black Haitian General defeated him in battle?

A. *Pierre Dominique Toussaint L'Ouverture*

■

Q. Who was the first Black to be enshrined in the United States Capitol Rotunda?

A. *Martin Luther King, Jr.*

Q. Who was the first American to die for American independence in the Revolutionary War?

A. *Crispus Attucks*

Q. What two Presidents' birthdays are observed during Black History Month?

A. *Presidents Lincoln & Washington*

Q. President Benjamin Harrison appointed what man as Minister Resident and Consul General to the Republic of Haiti in 1889?

A. *Frederick Douglass*

Q. This Black civilization of Persia existed around 2900 B.C. and is considered to be older than Ethiopia and Egypt. Who were they?

A. *Elam*

Q. In 3730 B.C., this Black man completed the Great Pyramid, which is 451 feet high, covers 31 acres, has 2,500,000 blocks of granite, and took 100,000 men thirty years to build. Name him.

A. *Cheops*

·

Q. This man was the third President of the United States, the father of the Declaration of Independence, and parented a large number of Mulatto children. Who is he?

A. *Thomas Jefferson*

·

Q. This sacred Indian river of India is named after the Great king of Ethiopia, who conquered Asia as far as this river flows. Name him.

A. *Ganges*

·

Q. His Ethiopian portraits show him as a Negro. Who is Imhotep of ancient Egypt said to be?

A. *The Father of Medicine*

·

Q. This European leader planned to solve the color problem in Haiti by making it legal for each man to take three wives: one white, one mulatto, and one Black. Who was he?

A. *Napoleon*

■

Q. This celestial saint of Germany is said to have been pure Negro. His picture is in many German cathedrals and museums, sometimes with the German eagle on his head. Who is he?

A. *Saint Maruice of Aganum*

■

Q. In 1863, the Emancipation Proclamation was signed by which President?

A. *Abraham Lincoln*

■

Q. On November 15, 218 B.C., this full-blooded Negro conquered territory in Spain and France. His military tactics are still taught in many military academies in England, France, Germany, and the United States. Who is he?

A. *Abraham Hannibal*

■

Q. In 1818, this Black man ascended to the throne of Sweden as Charles XIV and is known as the founder of the royal family of Sweden. Who was he?

A. *Jean Baptiste Jules Bernadotte*

■

Q. Who was the Black man who led slave revolts against the United States to free millions of slaves in the 1800s?

A. *Nat Turner*

■

Q. What president stated on many occasions, "Without the aid of the Negro, there might have been no United States," and stated it would be "impossible to win the war against the South without the Negro"?

A. *Abraham Lincoln*

■

Q. What president, in 1913, introduced segregation into federal government agencies?

A. *Woodrow Wilson*

■

Q. Who was the only woman to serve on President Roosevelt's Black Cabinet?

A. *Mary McCleod Bethune*

·

Q. Benjamin T. Montgomery purchased this confederate president's plantation and is said to have become the best cotton planter in Mississippi. Can you name this confederate president?

A. *Jefferson Davis*

·

Q. This blind writer, composer and singer was very instrumental in making the birthday of The Rev. Dr. Martin Luther King, Jr. a national holiday. Name him.

A. *Stevie Wonder*

·

Q. Who was the first Black to head the prestigious Ford Foundation?

A. *Franklin A. Thomas*

·

Q. Who was the first Black American to appear on a United States coin?

A. *Booker T. Washington*

Q. Who was the first Black person to place the American flag at the North Pole?

A. *Matthew Henson*

Q. The late director of the FBI, J. Edgar Hoover, called this man "the most notorious liar in the United States." Who was he talking about?

A. *Martin Luther King, Jr.*

Q. Who was the first Black to have his or her own TV show?

A. *Nat King Cole*

Countries

Q. What country was responsible for the European slave trade?

A. *Portugal*

Q. How many nations have honored Martin Luther King, Jr. by placing his picture on a postage stamp?

A. *Thirty-five*

Q. Which country dedicated the Martin Luther King, Jr. Memorial Forest, in his memory?

A. *Israel*

Q. The Falashas, or Negro Jews, called themselves "The chosen people," or the original Jews. In which country did they live?

A. *Ethiopia*

Q. The oldest and most noted statue in the world bears the face of a Negro. Name it.

A. *The Sphinx of Gizeh*

Q. Haile Selassie was emperor of what great African country?

A. *Ethiopia*

Q. He was known as the world's greatest musician: He was sometimes referred to as "The Black Spaniard."

A. *Beethoven (the man who freed music, R.H. Schauffler and race and civilization Fredrick Hertz)*

■

Q. This Black civilization of Persia existed around 2900 B.C. and is considered to be older than Ethiopia and Egypt.

A. *Elam*

■

Q. Victor (189-199), A.D. Melchiades (311-312), and St. Gelasius (469 A.D.) were what?

A. *All African Popes of Rome*

■

Q. In 1879, Cetewayo, King of what South Africa land, massacred an entire British army?

A. *Zulu*

■

Q. From 1440 – 1773, thousands of Guinean Blacks were imported into what part of the world?

A. *Europe*

■

Cities and States

Q. The state of Virginia elected this Black American as the nation's first Black governor.

A. *Douglas Wilder*

■

Q. In 1989, he became New York's first Black mayor.

A. *David N. Dinkins*

■

Q. Jamestown was the first place the slaves landed in America. What state is Jamestown in?

A. *Virginia*

■

Q. What was the first state to segregate its phone booths?

A. *Oklahoma*

■

Q. In 1664, which colony passed a law stating that any white woman who married a Negro should serve the master of such slave for life?

A. *Maryland*

■

Q. What was the first state to send an all-Black combat unit to fight in the Civil War?

A. *Kansas*

■

Q. The colony of Massachusetts was the first to do what?

A. *Legalize slavery*

■

Q. In 1783, which was the first state to abolish slavery?

A. *Vermont*

■

Q. What was the second state to abolish slavery?

A. *New Hampshire*

■

Q. In 1670, what colony passed a law that forbade Black people buying from white people?

A. *Virginia*

•

Q. The Oklahoma Constitution violated the 15th Amendment of the U.S. Constitution by giving illiterate whites, but denying illiterate Blacks, the right to vote. What was it called?

A. *The Grandfather Clause*

•

Q. What city were the first African slaves put ashore at in 1619?

A. *Jamestown*

•

Q. He was born Lincoln Perry in 1902 at Key West, Florida. He became one of the first Black film millionaires after signing with 20th Century Fox in 1926.

A. *Stepin Fetchit*

•

INVENTORS

Q. What Black American invented the automatic car washer?

A. *Richard B. Spikes*

Q. What Black inventor invented the railway telegraph device?

A. *Granville T. Woods*

Q. What Black inventor received the patent for inventing the guitar?

A. *R. F. Flemming, Jr.*

Q. This great inventor set up the first blood bank in England and in the United States, and is credited for developing the technique for separating blood plasma. Who was this great inventor?

A. *Dr. Charles Drew*

Q. What man invented automatic lubrication systems in 1872?

A. *Elijah J. McCoy*

Q. The invention of the shoe-lasting machine revolutionized the shoe industry. Who was the inventor?

A. *Jan Matzeliger*

Q. He refused to patent his discoveries, saying "God gave them to me, Why should I claim to own them?" Who was he?

A. *George Washington Carver*

Q. What machine did Jan Matzeliger invent that revolutionized the shoe industry?

A. *Shoe-Lasting Machine*

Q. What Black cowboy invented bulldogging?

A. *Bill Pickett*

Q. What female Black American patented the brush in 1898?

A. *L. D. Newman*

Q. Who invented the air brake?

A. *Granville T. Woods*

Q. What Black man invented the oil derrick?

A. *J. W. Benton (patent 1900)*

Q. Name the Black American who invented the riding saddle for horses.

A. *W. D. Davis*

Q. Who was the Black American who patented the fountain pen in 1890?

A. *W. B. Purvis*

Q. Who invented the method of inexpensively refining sugar?

A. *Norbert Rillieux*

Q. He was known as the "Black Edison" of the early 1900s, with over fifty inventions to his credit, and was responsible for the third rail now used in subway systems. Who was this great inventor?

A. *Granville T. Woods*

Q. Who invented the gas mask used as a breathing device for fire fighters?

A. *Garrett A. Morgan*

Q. The automatic gear shift was invented by what Black American?

A. *Richard B. Spikes*

Q. Name the Black American who invented the railroad car coupling device.

A. *Andrew Beard*

Q. This man invented the bridle bit for horses. Name him.

A. *L. F. Brown*

Q. What Black American invented the oil lubricating cup?

A. *Elijah J. McCoy*

Q. What Black invented the stop light?

A. *Garrett A. Morgan*

Q. Who patented the lawn sprinkler?

A. *Elijah J. McCoy*

Q. What Black man invented the starter generator?

A. *Frederick M. Jones*

Q. The phrase "The Real McCoy" is related to which Black inventor?

A. *Elijah J. McCoy*

Q. What Black American patented the elevator?

A. *A. Miles*

Q. What Black American invented the fire escape for upper floors of burning buildings?

A. *J. B. Winters*

·

Q. This great inventor is well known for single-handedly revolutionizing the agricultural industry by extracting hundred of products from the peanut, sweet potato, soy bean, and pecan. Who was he?

A. *George Washington Carver*

·

Q. What Black American designed the first portable X-Ray machine?

A. *Frederick M. Jones*

·

Q. What Black inventor and draftsman was the chief draftsman for both General Electric and Westinghouse?

A. *Lewis H. Latimer*

·

Q. Who invented the cotton planter machine?

A. *Henry Blair*

·

Q. What Black American invented the directional signal on cars?

A. *Richard B. Spikes*

Q. Who was the Black American who patented the mechanical potato digger?

A. *P. D. Smith*

Q. The first clock made in America was made in 1754 by whom?

A. *Benjamin Banneker*

Q. George Olden was the first Black man to design this United States product. What was it?

A. *Postage stamp*

Q. Name the Black American who patented the telephone transmitter.

A. *Granville T. Woods*

Q. What man discovered over 300 uses for the peanut?

A. *George Washington Carver*

•

Q. What Black American invented the map?

A. *T. W. Stewart*

•

Q. Who invented the sugar cane planter?

A. *Leonard Julien (The Julien Planter)*

•

Q. This Black American invented the beer keg. Name him.

A. *Richard B. Spikes*

•

Q. Name the Black American who invented the pencil sharpener.

A. *J. L. Love*

•

Q. The first corn harvester was invented by whom?

A. *Henry Blair*

•

Q. What Black woman invented the ironing board?

A. *Sarah Boone*

Q. This great inventor sent his personal representative to Tuskegee University to ask George Washington Carver to join him in Orange, New Jersey, as an associate. Who was he?

A. *Thomas Edison*

Q. This Black American invented the thermostat and temperature control system.

A. *Frederick M. Jones*

Q. This Black American patented the lock in 1889. Can you name him?

A. *W. A. Martin*

Q. Which Black American is credited with 23 lubrication inventions?

A. *Elijah J. McCoy*

Q. In 1933, this Black American invented the automatic transmission. Who was he?

A. *Richard B. Spikes*

Q. Name the Black American who patented the lawn mower in 1899.

A. *J. A. Burr*

Q. What Black inventor is credited with 25 electrical inventions?

A. *Granville T. Woods*

Q. What Black American invented the incandescent lamp?

A. *Lewis Latimer*

Q. What is J. W. Reed noted for?

A. *He invented the dough roller and kneader, which revolutionized the baking industry.*

Q. What is P. Walker noted for?

A. *He invented the machine for cleaning cotton seeds*

Q. In 1957, this Black American made it possible for perishables to be transported by railroad boxcars.

A. *Frederick M. Jones*

•

Q. Who was the inventor who created the test to detect syphilis?

A. *Dr. William Hinton*

•

Q. The earliest known (pre-Civil War) patent granted to a Black was for a utility patent for an invention on dry scouring of clothes.

A. *Thomas A. Jennings (March 3, 1821)*

•

Q. On October 14, 1834, this Black man received two utility patents on a seed planter; and another on a cotton planter on August 31, 1836.

A. *Henry Blair*

•

Q. While in Leavenworth prison for violating the Mann Act, this Black man received a patent on an improved type of monkeywrench.

A. *John Arthur Johnson, (Jack Johnson, Boxer)*

Q. He received patents on a cosmetic and a process of producing paints and stains.

A. *George Washington Carver*

Q. This great inventor invented the vacuum pan, which revolutionized the sugar industry.

A. *Norbert Rillieux*

Q. This Black man invented the "incineraid," a device that controls smoke pollution, and the electradyne paint spray gun. Some of his inventions have been licensed to Sherwin-Williams Paint Company.

A. *Meredith C. Gourdine (Dr. Meredith C. Gourdine won a silver medal in broad jump at the 1952 Olympics)*

Q. This Black woman was one of the first to receive a patent for her invention of the folding cabinet bed.

A. *Sarah E. Goode (July 14, 1885)*

Q. Records show her to be the second Black woman to receive a patent for her invention for a gong and signal chair. It was used in the U.S. House of Representatives.

A. *Miriam E. Benjamin (July 17, 1888)*

Q. This famous Black woman accumulated great wealth from her inventions on cosmetics. In 1910, she constructed a research laboratory that produced facial creams, hair preparations, and the hair-straightening comb.

A. *Sara Breedlove Walker (Madam C.J. Walker)*

Q. Born in 1731, this Black man will be remembered for his invention of an almanac and a clock. Beside his agricultural pursuits, he devoted his time to scientific and mechanical studies.

A. *Benjamin Banneker (born Maryland, 1731 to 1806)*

Q. Born James Forten of Philadelphia, Penn., he invited an apparatus for managing what?

A. *Sails — 1766 to 1842*

Q. This Black man invented a machine for picking Oakum, which is used for caulking seams in wooden ships and packing pipe joints.

A. *Robert Benjamin Lewis (born 1802 in Gardiner, Maine)*

•

Q. Along with his brother Lyates, this Black man's inventions relate principally to electronic subjects; telegraphic and telephonic instruments, electric railways and general systems of electrical control, and several patents on means for transmitting telegraphic messages between moving trains.

A. *Granville T. Woods*

•

Q. He invented a machine for making paper bags the fountain pen, and earned patents on the electric railways.

A. *William B. Purvis (Philadelphia)*

•

Q. This Black man invented a device for automatically playing the piano. His company is said to be one of the largest corporations of its kind.

A. *Joseph Hunter Dickinson (New Jersey)*

•

MEDICINE

Q. In 1893, this medical pioneer was the first to perform open heart surgery. Who was he?

A. *Dr. Daniel Hale Williams*

Q. Dr. William Hinton created the test to detect what well-known disease?

A. *Syphilis*

Q. Who was the first Black to receive his Doctor of Medical Science degree from Columbia University in Indianola, Iowa?

A. *Dr. Charles Drew*

Q. Who was the first Black woman physician?

A. *Rebecca Cole*

Q. Who was the first Black man to become a physician in America?

A. *James Derham*

Q. Why was the National Medical Association formed?

A. *Because Blacks were not allowed to join the American Medical Association*

•

Q. When was the National Medical Association formed?

A. *1895*

•

Q. Dr. Daniel Hale Williams, a Chicago surgeon, was the first to perform a successful operation on the human heart. When did he die?

A. *1931*

•

Q. Who was Dr. Williams's patient for the heart operation?

A. *James Cornish*

•

Q. Who is the founder of Chicago Providence Hospital?

A. *Dr. Daniel Hale Williams*

•

MILITARY

Army

Q. Who was the first Black woman to become a general in the army?

A. *Hazel Johnson (nurses corp)*

Q. Who was the first Black woman to hold the rank of Colonel in the army, and who also was its first chief nurse?

A. *Margaret E. Bailey*

Q. Who was the first Black to become an Army General?

A. *Brig. General B. O. Davis, Sr.*

Q. Who was the first Black American to graduate from the West Point Military Academy?

A. *William O. Flipper*

Q. Roscoe Robinson, Jr. became the first Black Four-Star General of what branch of service?

A. *U.S. Army*

Q. Who was the first Black to be confirmed to the Cabinet as Secretary of the Army?

A. *Clifford Alexander, Jr.*

Q. Who was the first Black man to be commissioned as a warrant officer for the National Guard?

A. *Thomas J. Hargis, Jr.*

Air Force

Q. Who was the first Black to become an Air Force General?

A. *Lt. General B. O. Davis, Jr.*

Q. Who was the first Black selected for Air Force Pilot training?

A. *George S. Robert*

Q. Who was the first Black Air Force Squadron leader?

A. *Major Joseph DuBois Alsberry*

Q. How long did Major Joseph Alsberry serve in the Air Force?

A. *20 years*

Q. Where was Major Joseph Alsberry born?

A. *Stillwater, Oklahoma*

Q. Who became the first four star general in the Air Force?

A. *General Chappy James*

Navy

Q. Brenda Robinson was the first Black female pilot in what branch of service?

A. *United States Navy*

Q. Who was the first Black to become an Admiral in the Navy?

A. *Samuel L. Gravely, Jr.*

Q. Who was the first Black navy pilot?

A. *Ensign Jesse Brown*

Q. Wesley A. Brown became the first Black graduate of this military academy.

A. *Annapolis Naval Academy*

Q. Who was the first Black woman Commander in the United States Navy Corps?

A. *Hazel P. McCree*

Marines

Q. John Earl Rudder became the first Black officer of what branch of service?

A. *U. S. Marine Corps*

Q. In 1979, this man became the first Black General of the Marine Corps. Who is he?

A. *Frank E. Petersen, Jr.*

Q. After what war was the presidential order signed banning segregation of the armed forces?

A. *World War II*

Q. In 1984, Lt. Robert Goodman was rescued by what American leader?

A. *The Rev. Jesse L. Jackson*

Q. Who was the first Black to become chairman of the Joint Chiefs of Staff?

A. *Cullen Powell*

OCCUPATIONS

Q. Paul R. Williams is the architect of record who designed a famous hotel in Beverly Hills, California. What is the hotel?

A. *Beverly Wilshire*

•

Q. What was Paul Cuffee's occupation?

A. *Shipbuilder (1790)*

•

Q. Who is the Black Chocolate Chip Cookie King?

A. *Famous Amos*

•

Q. What is Rod Carew's occupation?

A. *Baseball player*

•

Q. What do Roy Campanella, Willie McCovey, and Lou Brock have in common?

A. *Baseball players*

•

Q. What is Bob Gibson's occupation?

A. *Baseball pitcher (one of seven to unanimously win*

the Cy Young Award)

▪

Q. What is Lynette Woodard's occupation?

A. *Basketball/Athletics*

▪

Q. What is the occupation of Wilt Chamberlain?

A. *Basketball player (National Basketball Association leader in rebounds)*

▪

Q. Who is Wilt Chamberlain?

A. *Basketball player*

▪

Q. What is Bill Russell's occupation?

A. *Pro basketball player (Celtics, 1966)*

▪

Q. What is Don King's occupation?

A. *Fight promoter*

▪

Q. Who is Ethel Waters?

A. *Singer/actress*

▪

Q. What was Henry Armstrong's occupation?

A. Boxer

·

Q. Who is Sugar Ray Robinson?

A. *A boxer*

·

Q. Who was Paul Robeson?

A. *An actor/singer*

·

Q. What was Lewis H. Latimer's occupation?

A. *Inventor and draftsman*

·

Q. What were the occupations of G.T. Sampson and Frederick M. Jones?

A. *Inventors*

·

Q. What was Harriet Tubman's occupation?

A. *Nurse*

·

Q. What is the occupation of Samuel L. Kountz?

A. *Doctor (he discovered the tolerable drug dosage of a drug used to prevent the rejection of transplanted human organs)*

■

Q. Singer, actress, author, and the first Black pinup girl during World War II.

A. *Lena Horne*

■

POLITICAL SCIENCE

Q. Mary McCleod Bethune was the only Black woman to serve on this President's Black Cabinet. Name him.

A. *Franklin D. Roosevelt*

Q. He first gained national recognition as a contender for the democratic Presidential nomination in 1984. Name this son of a sharecropper.

A. *The Rev. Jesse L. Jackson*

Q. Who was the first Black woman to be admitted to the United States Congress in 1968?

A. *Shirley Chisholm*

Q. Who was the first Black woman to be a candidate for the Democratic Presidential nomination?

A. *Shirley Chisholm*

Q. She was the first Black keynote speaker at a 1976 national Democratic party convention. Name her.

A. *Barbara Jordan*

•

Q. Who was the first Black to be elected Mayor of Birmingham, Alabama?

A. *Richard Arrington*

•

Q. Who was the first Black to become the President of the United States Conference of Mayors?

A. *Kenneth Gibson, Mayor of Newark, New Jersey*

•

Q. Who was the first Black to be elected Mayor of Prichard, Alabama?

A. *A. J. Cooper*

•

Q. Who was the first Black to be elected Mayor of Tuskegee, Alabama?

A. *Johnny Ford*

•

Q. In 1975, this Black was appointed chief justice of a federal court.

A. *James Benton Parsons*

•

Q. Who was the first Black to be elected Mayor of New Orleans, Louisiana?

A. *Ernest N. Morial*

•

Q. Who was the first Black to be elected Mayor of Los Angeles?

A. *Thomas Bradley*

•

Q. Who was the first Black to be elected Mayor of Atlanta, Georgia?

A. *Maynard Jackson*

•

Q. Who was the first Black to be elected Mayor of Detroit, Michigan?

A. *Coleman Young*

•

Q. What committee was Democrat William L. Dawson the first Black to chair in Congress?

A. *Congressional*

■

Q. Who was the first Black to be sworn into the United States House of Representatives?

A. *Joseph H. Rainey, in 1870*

■

Q. What was the first city to elect a Black mayor?

A. *Cleveland, Ohio*

■

Q. Who was appointed United States Marshal of Washington, D.C. by President Rutherford B. Hayes in 1877?

A. *Frederic Douglas*

■

Q. Who was the Black man who played a key role in exposing the Watergate conspiracy?

A. *Frank Wills*

■

Q. Edith Sampson was America's first Black woman to be appointed as alternate delegate to what world organization?

A. *The United Nations*

Q. Who was the first Black astronaut?

A. *Major Robert H. Lawrence, Jr.*

Q. Who was the first Black high-ranking officer of the United Nations?

A. *Dr. Ralph J. Bunche*

Q. Under the Reagan administration, he became the chairman of the Civil Rights Commission.

A. *Clarence Pendelton*

Q. Walter Washington was the first Black mayor of what city?

A. *Washington, D.C.*

Q. Who was the first Black to head a U.S. embassy in Europe?

A. *Clifton R. Wharton, Sr.*

Q. Who was the first Black to be appointed to the Federal court?

A. *James B. Parsons*

Q. Who was the first Black to be elected to the U.S. Senate?

A. *Edward W. Brooke*

Q. Who was the first Black to become a presidential cabinet member?

A. *Robert Weaver*

Q. What was Robert Weaver's title?

A. *Secretary of Housing & Urban Development*

Q. Who was the first Black woman to be appointed to the federal bench?

A. *Constance Baker Motley*

Q. Who was the first Black to serve as Mayor of a major United States city?

A. *Carl B. Stokes*

·

Q. Who was the first Black to become Mayor of Chicago?

A. *Harold Washington*

·

Q. Jane Matilda Bolin was the first Black woman to be appointed Judge to the Court of Domestic Relations. From what city was she appointed?

A. *New York City*

·

Q. Who was the first Black to be appointed to the United States Supreme Court?

A. *Thurgood Marshall*

·

Q. In 1962, he was the first Black to be elected congressman from the state of California. Who was he?

A. *Agustus Hawkins*

·

Q. Who was the first Black woman to become a federal Judge?

A. *Constance Baker Motley*

Q. Who preceded John Jacobs as executive director of the National Urban League?

A. *Vernon Jordan*

Q. What Black woman successfully led the fight for a national holiday in honor of her late husband?

A. *Coretta Scott King*

Q. Who was the first Black woman ambassador and the first Black woman Cabinet member?

A. *Patricia Harris*

Q. What congressman from Chicago was the first Black to head a standing committee of Congress?

A. *Congressman William L. Dawson*

Q. Who was the founder of "People United to Save Humanity"?

A. *The Rev. Jesse L. Jackson*

Q. Who was the first Black woman from the state of New York elected to Congress?

A. *Shirley Chisholm*

Q. Who was the first Black woman that was elected to a state legislature?

A. *Crystal Bird Fauset*

Q. After the Civil War, what president vetoed a bill giving full rights to free slaves?

A. *President Andrew Johnson*

Q. This man was the first Black nominated for president by a major national party. Who is this favorite son from the District of Columbia?

A. *Reverend Channing E. Phillips*

Q. From what state was Crystal Bird Fauset elected to the Legislature?

A. *Pennsylvania*

Q. Frederick Douglass was an advisor to what President of the United States?

A. *Abraham Lincoln*

Q. Who is the only Black American to have a memorial on federal parkland?

A. *Mary McCleod Bethune*

Q. Who organized the first Pan-African Congress in 1919?

A. *W. E. B. Du Bois*

Q. James Farmer is the founder of what organization?

A. *CORE — Congress of Racial Equality*

Q. Who represented the Harlem district in Congress for 25 years?

A. *Adam Clayton Powell, Jr.*

Q. What was the reason for the Civil Rights Act, which was passed by Congress in 1964?

A. *Anti-Housing Discrimination*

Q. What organization was started by Huey P. Newton and Bobby G. Seal in the 1960s?

A. *The Black Panthers*

Q. In Washington, D.C., the American Colonization Society was formed for what?

A. *To send Blacks back to Africa*

Q. Which Black man created the Universal Negro Improvement Association in the 1920s?

A. *Marcus Garvey*

Q. In 1925, this union leader organized the Pullman porters and maids, to become one of the most influential leaders in the labor movement. Name him.

A. *A. Phillip Randolph*

Q. On which U.S. stamp does the picture of Mary McCleod Bethune appear?

A. *22-cent*

•

Q. Name the speech in which Booker T. Washington urged Blacks to accept segregation in exchange for economic...

A. *The Atlanta Compromise*

•

Q. Who was the first woman to be elected to the National Institute of Arts and Letters?

A. *Gwendolyn Brooks*

•

Q. Who was the first woman and first Black woman to be elected president of the National Bar Association?

A. *Arnette Hubbard*

•

Q. What was the first Black company to be listed on the American Stock Exchange?

A. *Johnson Products, Co.*

•

POLITICAL SCIENCE   ■ 85

Q. In the 67-year history of the Tournament of Roses parade, she is the first Black to become its rose queen. Name her.

A. *Kristina Smith*

•

Q. Prince Hall was the first Grand Master of what organization?

A. *Black Masons*

•

Q. In 1972, he became the first Black to join the board of directors of the New York Stock Exchange. Name him.

A. *Jerome H. Holland*

•

Q. When is Martin Luther King, Jr. Day?

A. *Third Monday in January*

•

Q. Who was the first Black to hold a commercial pilot's license?

A. *Charles A. Anderson*

•

Q. Maggie L. Walker is the first woman to hold what position in America?

A. *Bank President*

·

Q. Who was the first Black to sculpt a United States coin?

A. *Isaac Scott Hathaway*

·

Q. Who is said to be America's first Black millionaire?

A. *William Alexander Liedesdroff*

·

Q. Who was the first Black woman to be crowned Miss Black American in 1969?

A. *Gloria Smith*

·

Q. Manufacturer of hair preparations, she is reported to be the first Black woman to become a millionaire. A pioneer Black business leader, who was she?

A. *Madame C. J. Walker*

·

Q. Who was the first Black American killed in an American space shuttle?

A. *Ronald E. McNair*

Q. Who was the first Black American to fly into outer space?

A. *Lt. Col. Guion S. Bluford, Jr.*

Q. Who was the first Black to win the title of Miss America?

A. *Vanessa Williams*

Q. On what United States stamp does the picture of Jackie Robinson appear?

A. *15-cent*

Q. Roy Wilkins was director of what organization in 1954?

A. *NAACP*

Q. What part of Africa did Black Americans come from?

A. *West Africa*

．

Q. The United States Supreme Court ruled that a State of Virginia law banning what was unconstitutional?

A. *Interracial marriage*

．

Q. When was W E R D founded?

A. *October 3rd, 1949*

．

Q. This lady died May 1, 1955. She was affectionately known as America's First Black Lady, founder of the National Council of Negro Women, and was special advisor to Presidents Roosevelt and Truman. Who was she?

A. *Mary McCleod Bethune*

．

Q. This woman was a seamstress by trade and an activist who refused to give her seat to a white man on a Montgomery, Alabama bus. Who is she?

A. *Rosa Parks*

■

Q. W E R D was the first Black-owned and operated radio station in what United States city?

A. *Atlanta*

■

Q. What is the period after the Civil War known as? Some say it is when true democracy existed.

A. *Reconstruction Era*

■

Q. Federal Public Law 98-144 is the congressional law making what a legal holiday?

A. *Martin Luther King, Jr. Day*

■

Q. During the Civil War, this Black woman became the first and the last American woman to lead American soldiers in battle. Under her direction a band of 300 Black soldiers destroyed millions of dollars worth of enemy property. Who was she?

A. *Harriet Tubman*

Q. In the 1960s, James Farmer, a Methodist minister, began what?

A. *The Freedom Rides*

Q. In 1969, a shocking sermon demanding almost $500 million in payment to Blacks for economic injustices under slavery was delivered. What was this sermon called?

A. *The Black Manifesto*

Q. Who was publicly debated to have been a Black American, this according to a historian?

A. *Warren G. Harding (historian-J. A. Rogers)*

Q. Harper's Ferry, Virginia is where whose anti-slavery revolt began?

A. *John Brown's*

•

Q. What Black Revolutionary War hero was recognized on a 10-cent stamp during the 1976 Bicentennial?

A. *Salem Poor*

•

Q. For what fugitive slave does a historical monument stand at the courthouse in St. Louis, Missouri?

A. *Dred Scott*

•

Q. What labor leader forced President Franklin D. Roosevelt to end hiring discrimination in defense plants during World War II and also threatened to march on Washington?

A. *A. Phillip Randolph*

•

Q. In the 1600s, the colony of Maryland became the first to pass laws against what?

A. *Interracial marriages*

•

Q. What amendment to the Constitution was accepted by the Confederate States, in order for them to be accepted back into the union?

A. *The 14th Amendment*

∎

Q. Who is Los Angeles's first Black man to be a four-term elected mayor?

A. *Mayor Tom Bradley*

∎

Q. Who was the first Black woman appointed President of the New York State Civil Service Commission?

A. *Ersa Hines Poston*

∎

Q. Where was Ersa Hines Poston born?

A. *Paducah, Kentucky*

∎

PUBLISHING

Q. The first Black newspaper was published in 1827 by whom?

A. *John B. Russwurm and Samuel E. Cornish*

■

Q. Name three of the seven Black newspapers created in the 1920s.

A. *The Colored American, The Elevator, The Peoples Press, The Clarion, The National Reformer, The Mirror of the Times, and The Herald of Freedom*

■

Q. What New York newspaper first capitalized the N in Negro?

A. *The New York Times*

■

Q. November 1945 was the date this Black magazine went on sale.

A. *Ebony Magazine*

■

Q. She wrote a series of articles in the *Negro Digest* that gave the publication its rise to fame. Name her.

A. *Eleanor Roosevelt*

■

Q. What was the name of the articles written by Eleanor Roosevelt?

A. *If I Were a Negro*

■

Q. Kunta Kinte was the character in what Alex Hailey book?

A. *Roots*

■

Q. John Russwurm was co-founder of the first Black newspaper. Can you name it?

A. *Freedom's Journal*

■

Q. What magazine hit the stands in 1945? It was about Blacks, for Blacks.

A. *Ebony*

■

Q. The first abolitionist newspaper was printed in what year?

A. *1827*

■

Q. What is the oldest Black continuous publication?

A. *The Crisis...NAACP*

■

Q. What magazine is called "the magazine for today's Black woman"?

A. *Essence*

■

RELIGION

Q. Who was the first woman to become an ordained bishop of the Episcopal church?

A. *Barbara Harris in February 1989*

Q. Name the first Black to be ordained Bishop.

A. *Absalom Jones*

Q. What is the first independent Black church body in America?

A. *Methodist*

Q. The African Methodist Church was founded by what Black American?

A. *Richard Allen*

Q. Who founded the Southern Christian Leadership conference?

A. *The Rev. Dr. Martin Luther King, Jr.*

Q. What Philadelphia Baptist minister created the Opportunities Industrialization Center?

A. *Reverend Leon Sullivan*

■

Q. The Underground railroad was established by what religious organization?

A. *Quakers*

■

Football

Q. Who played professional football for the Oakland Raiders before becoming an actor?

A. *Carl Weathers*

■

Q. What Chicago Bears star is known as the "Refrigerator"?

A. *William Perry*

■

Q. Mercury Morris played for what professional football team?

A. *Miami Dolphins*

■

Q. Jim Brown began his football career with what team?

A. *Cleveland Browns*

■

Q. What football great is credited with breaking Jim Brown's rushing records?

A. *Walter Payton*

•

Q. With what team do you associate Walter Payton?

A. *Chicago Bears*

•

Q. Name the first Black Heisman trophy winner.

A. *Ernie Davis*

•

Q. What Black football coach has the winningest record in history?

A. *Eddie Robinson (surpassed the NFL record of George Halas)*

•

Q. Who was the first Black referee in the history of football?

A. *Johnny Greer*

•

Q. He became the first to rush for over 2,000 yards in a single season. Who is this football great?

A. *O. J. Simpson*

■

Q. What football star was inducted into the Football Hall of Fame in 1971? He was the alltime NFL leader in touchdowns (126) and had a career yardage of 12,312.

A. *Jim Brown*

■

Q. This football player lives up to the true meaning of mean; he was a member of the famous steel curtain. Who is the defensive lineman?

A. *Mean Joe Greene*

■

Q. Who was the first Pro-Football head coach?

A. *Willie Wood, in 1975*

■

Q. Marion Motley was drafted by what team?

A. *Cleveland Browns, in 1950*

■

Q. Before his career with the Dallas Cowboys, this athlete was known as the world's fastest human. Who is he?

A. *Bob Hayes*

■

Q. Who was the first inductee into the Pro Football Hall of Fame?

A. *Emlen Tunnell*

■

Baseball

Q. What famous baseball star became the first Black manager of a major league baseball team?

A. *Frank Robinson*

■

Q. Who was the first Black to play major league baseball?

A. *Jackie Robinson*

■

Q. What year did Jackie Robinson enter the National League to break the color barrier?

A. *1947*

■

Q. Who became a major league rookie at 42 years of age?

A. *Satchel Paige*

●

Q. Not only did this man break Babe Ruth's home run record, he broke his runs batted in. Who was he?

A. *Hank Aaron*

●

Q. What Black baseball player beat Ty Cobb's stolen bases record with 893?

A. *Lou Brock*

●

Q. This man was the National League's first Black pitcher and the winner of the Cy Young award. Who is he?

A. *Don Newcombe*

●

Q. Elston Howard was the first Black man to win what award in the American League, in 1963?

A. *Most Valuable Player*

●

Q. Who was the first Black to lead an NCAA baseball team to a Division title?

A. *John Thompson/Coach*

■

Q. What league did Josh Gibson play for?

A. *Homestead Gray Negro League*

■

Q. What baseball team did Ernie Banks play for?

A. *Chicago Cubs*

■

Q. What were the Kansas City Monarchs?

A. *An all-Black baseball club*

■

Q. What man is an eight-time batting champion?

A. *Rod Carew*

■

Q. Emmett Ashford was the first Black to become what?

A. *Major league umpire*

■

Q. Name the man who was the American League's first Black pitcher to win the Cy Young Award.

A. *Vida Blue*

■

Q. Who was the first baseball Hall of Fame inductee to appear on a United States postage stamp?

A. *Jackie Robinson*

■

Q. Larry Doby was a Black major league baseball player who played for what league?

A. *American*

■

Q. After breaking Babe Ruth's major league baseball record, he became the all-time home run king when he hit no. 715 against the Los Angeles Dodgers. Who is he?

A. *Henry (Hank) Aaron*

■

Q. During the 1977 World Series, this great baseball star hit three homers against the Los Angeles Dodgers to win the series. Who is he?

A. *Reggie Jackson*

■

Q. This baseball star was known for his over-the-shoulder catch. Who is he?

A. *Willie Mays*

■

Q. What team did Willie Mays play for?

A. *San Francisco Giants*

■

Q. Who was the last baseball team to integrate their team?

A. *Boston Red Sox*

■

Q. Who became the first baseball star to steal one hundred bases in a season?

A. *Maury Wills*

■

Q. Who is the youngest pitcher to win 20 games in modern baseball history?

A. *Dwight Gooden*

■

Q. Who was the first Black to become a major league umpire?

A. *Emmett Ashford*

■

Q. In what baseball league did the first Black umpire appear?

A. *American League*

Q. After Jackie Robinson's entry into the National League, what American league team was first to play Black players?

A. *Cleveland Indians*

Q. The Reggie Bar is named after what great baseball star?

A. *Reggie Jackson*

Q. What is Reggie Jackson's nickname?

A. *Mr. October*

Q. What was Jackie Robinson's true name?

A. *Jack Roosevelt*

Q. In World War II, Jackie Robinson held what rank?

A. *Lieutenant*

Q. On what United States stamp does the picture of Jackie Robinson appear?

A. *15-cent*

■

Basketball

Q. Who was the first Black American pro basketball coach?

A. *Bill Russell*

■

Q. What Los Angles Laker basketball player broke Jerry West's career playoff scoring record ?

A. *Kareem Abdul-Jabbar*

■

Q. How tall is Kareem Abdul-Jabbar?

A. *7 feet 2 inches*

■

Q. Who is the taller of the two — Wilt Chamberlain or Kareem Abdul-Jabbar?

A. *Kareem Abdul-Jabbar*

■

Q. Who played for Michigan State University before joining the Los Angeles Lakers?

A. *Earvin Magic Johnson*

Q. Kareem Abdul-Jabbar broke this basketball great's career-points-scored record in the National Basketball League.

A. *Wilt Chamberlain*

Q. Who was the National Basketball Association's first Black player?

A. *Bill Russell*

Q. What famous basketball player is known as Dr. J.?

A. *Julius Erving*

Q. Who was the first Black basketball coach to win an NCAA Division Championship?

A. *John Thompson — 1984*

Q. This man is referred to by his fans as the big "O". Who is this great basketball star?

A. *Oscar Robertson*

Q. What person was the Harlem Wizzards biggest attraction?

A. *George Bell*

Boxing

Q. Muhammad Ali became the Olympic champion in what division in 1960?

A. *Light Heavyweight Champion*

Q. Name the first Black to win the Welterweight title.

A. *Jersey Joe Walcott*

Q. Name the youngest man to win the heavyweight boxing title.

A. *Mike Tyson*

Q. What boxer is known as "The Hit Man"?

A. *Thomas Hearns*

•

Q. Who were the participants in the fight that was billed as the "Thriller in Manila"?

A. *Muhammad Ali and Joe Frazier*

•

Q. Who was the first to hold three world boxing championships at the same time?

A. *Henry Armstrong*

•

Q. Who won the Light-Heavyweight Olympic Gold Medal in Rome, in 1960?

A. *Muhammad Ali*

•

Q. Joe Gans was the first Black to hold what boxing title?

A. *Lightweight Title*

•

Q. Before he changed his name to Muhammad Ali, what was he called?

A. *Cassius Clay*

•

Q. Michael Spinks is the first Lightweight to win what boxing title?

A. *Heavyweight*

•

Q. Who was regarded as the greatest heavyweight champion of all times, and held the championship title from 1937 until his retirement in 1947, longer than any other heavyweight champion?

A. *Joe Louis*

•

Q. Name the man who, in their first meeting in the boxing ring, put heavyweight boxer Muhammad Ali on the canvas in the 15th round.

A. *Joe Frazier*

•

Q. What great champion defeated Muhammad Ali at Madison Square Garden on March 8, 1971?

A. *Joe Frazier*

•

Q. In 1890, George Dixon was the first Black to win what boxing title?

A. *Bantamweight Title*

•

Q. What great boxing champion defeated champion Sonny Liston for the heavyweight title on February 25th, 1964?

A. *Cassius Clay (Muhammad Ali)*

■

Q. What great welterweight champion reigned from 1946-1951? He was inducted into the Boxing Hall of Fame with a 25-year career with 174 wins and 109 KO's.

A. *Sugar Ray Robinson*

■

Q. How many times did Muhammad Ali win the heavyweight title?

A. *Three*

■

Q. Who was the first Black heavyweight boxing champion?

A. *Jack Johnson*

■

Q. Who is Walker Smith, Jr.?

A. *Sugar Ray Robinson*

■

Q. What was Joe Louis's real name?

A. *Joseph Louis Barrows*

Q. Tiger Flower was the first Black to hold what title?

A. *Middleweight Title*

Q. In 1810, Tom Molineaux was the first Black American boxing contender in what boxing division?

A. *Heavyweight*

Tennis

Q. Who was the first Black man to win a Wimbledon tennis title?

A. *Arthur Ashe*

Q. Who was the first Black American to enter the United States Open Tournament?

A. *John Shippen*

Q. Who was the first Black teenager to win the junior girls singles title at Wimbledon?

A. *Zina Garrison*

•

Q. Who was the first Black to win a tennis title at Wimbledon?

A. *Althea Gibson*

•

Q. Besides being the first Black man to win a Wimbledon championship, he was also the first to play on the Davis cup Tennis Team. Who is he?

A. *Arthur Ashe*

•

Olympics

Q. What Ethopian runner was the first to repeat as a marathon gold medalist in 1960 and 1964? He was also known for his victory as the first African ever to win a gold medal at the Olympic games.

A. *Abebe Bikila*

•

Q. Milton Campbell was the first Black to win what in the 1956 Olympics?

A. *Decathlon*

Q. What woman won three Olympic medals in the 1984 Olympics?

A. *Vallerie Brisco-Hooks*

Q. Who was the first Black to compete in the Olympics?

A. *George Poage*

Q. What track star won four gold medals at the Berlin Olympics before his death in 1966?

A. *Jesse Owens*

Q. Which Black American athlete won four gold medals at the 1984 Olympics?

A. *Carl Lewis*

Q. Who was the first Black to win an Olympic gold medal?

A. *DeHard Hubbard*

Q. Who was the great athlete who leaped to a record 29 feet, 2-1/2 inches in the long jump, October, 1968?

A. *Bob Beamon*

Q. What two Black athletes shook the world with the "Black Salute" as they stood during the medal ceremony with raised fists at the 1968 Mexico City Olympics?

A. *John Carlos & Tommie Smith*

Q. Who was the first Black woman named to a world figure skating team?

A. *Debbie Thomas*

Q. Who is Ralph H. Metcalfe?

A. *A Congressman, and former gold medal winner at the 1936 Berlin Olympics*

Golf

Q. Lee Elder was the first Black to play in what golf tournament?

A. *Masters*

■

Miscellaneous

Q. Tina Sloan was the first Black woman to compete on what national team?

A. *Lacrosse*

■

Q. In 1970, he was the first Black to win the Mr. America title.

A. *Chris Dickerson*

■

THEATRE

Q. Who won an Oscar for best supporting actor in *An Officer and a Gentleman*?

A. *Louis Gossett, Jr.*

●

Q. Darth Vadar's voice was that of whom?

A. *James Earl Jones*

●

Q. In 1939, this Black actress starred in the legendary movie *Gone With the Wind*. Name her.

A. *Hattie McDaniel*

●

Q. Who was the first Black to win an Academy Award?

A. *Hattie McDaniel*

●

Q. Name the Black actor who played opposite Diana Ross in *Lady Sings the Blues*.

A. *Billy Dee Williams*

●

Q. Who was the first Black male actor to win an Oscar Award?

A. *Sidney Poitier*

Q. This Black female comic was known as "Moms." Name her.

A. *Jackie "Moms" Mabley*

Q. Who wrote the musical soundtrack to the movie *Superfly*?

A. *Curtis Mayfield*

Q. What man is known as "The King of Tap Dancers"?

A. *Bill Robinson*

Q. Bandleader sometimes known as "Pops," the world knew him as "Satchmo."

A. *Louis Armstrong*

•

Q. He was sometimes called "The Wonder Boy." His credits include: *A Funny Thing Happened on the Way to the Forum, The River Niger, Come Back Charleston Blue,* and *Cotton Comes to Harlem.*

A. *Godfrey Cambridge*

•

Q. She became the first Black star to appear in her own network television series, *Julia.*

A. *Diahann Carroll (1954)*

•

Q. She became the first Black to be featured on the cover of *Life Magazine.* Born in Cleveland, Ohio, died in Hollywood, in 1965, of an overdose of drugs.

A. *Dorothy Dandridge*

•

Q. What was Amos 'n Andy in American history?

A. *Popular TV show that drew objecting views from civil rights organizations.*

•

Q. Who founded BET (Black Entertainment Television)?

A. *Robert L. Johnson*

•

Q. What role did Lou Gossett, Jr. play in the TV series "Roots"?

A. *Fiddler*

•

Q. What is Mr. T's real name?

A. *Lawrence Tayrue*

•

Q. In what TV series did Styme and Buckwheat star?

A. *The Little Rascals*

•

Q. What is comedian Redd Foxx's real name?

A. *John Sanford*

■

Q. Gary Coleman starred in what TV show?

A. *Different Strokes*

■

Q. Roger Mosley is the side kick on what TV show?

A. *Magnum, P.I.*

■

Q. What character does Roger Mosley play?

A. *T. C.*

■

Q. Sherman Hemsley starred in what TV series?

A. *The Jeffersons, and AMEN*

■

Q. Robert Guillaume starred on what TV series?

A. *Benson*

■

Q. Who is the only Black member of the CBS News 60-minutes team?

A. *Ed Bradley*

■

Q. An actor and comedian distinguished by his gravelly voice, was the sidekick on the Jack Benny Show.

A. *Eddie "Rochester" Anderson*

■

BLACK PATENTEES

James S. Adams, propelling means for aeroplanes, Oct. 1920

Virgie M. Ammons, fireplace damper actuating tool, Sept. 1975

Charles A. Bankhead, assembled composition printing, July 1963

James A. Bauer, coin-changer mechanism, Jan. 1970

Robert G. Bayless, encapsulation process and its product, Feb. 1971

Charles R. Beckley, folding chair, Dec. 1974

Alfred Benjamin, stainless steel scouring pads, June 1962

Henry Blair, seed planter, Oct. 1834; cotton planter, Aug. 1836

Peachy Booker, flying landing platform, Oct. 1961

Henrietta Bradbury, bed rack, May 1943; torpedo discharge means, Dec. 1945

James R. Briscoe, building blocks, with a side con. April, 1968

Phil Brooks, disposable syringe, April 1974

Henry T. Brown, combined isomerization and crack, reactivating hydro forming catalysts, Oct. 1968

Marie Van Brittan Brown, home security systems, etc., Dec. 1969

Paul L. Brown, spinable stringless top, Aug. 1970

Robert F. Bundy, signal generator, Dec. 1960

George R. Carruthers, image converter for detecting electromagnetic, etc., Nov. 1969

George Washington Carver, cosmetic, Jan. 1925, paint and stain and process, June 1925; process of producing paint, June 1927

John B. Christian, grease comp. for use at high temp. grease composition of fluorcarbon polymers, etc., Oct. 1970

Leander M. Coles, mortician's table, March 1974

Thomas L. Cosby, rotary machine closed-cycle energy conversion system, July 1969 and 1974

Donald J. Cotton, vertical liquid electrode, etc., Aug. 1977

Beatrice L. Cowans, embroidered fruit bowl wall hanging and kit, April 1977

Elbert L. Cox, presettable bistable circuits, Aug. 1967

Stephen H. Davis, load weighing and totaling device, etc., July 1943

Benjamin A. Dent, procedure entry for a data processor employing etc., Dec. 1970

Cortland O. Dugger, method for growing oxide, etc., July 1971

Clarence L. Elder, sweepstake programmer, Jan. 1971; non-capsizable container, Feb. 1968; bidirectional monitoring and control sys., Dec. 1976

Phillip E. Emile, transistorized gating circuit, May 1961; transistorized multivibrator circuit, Nov. 1961

Irvin S. Frye, adjustable shackle, Sept. 1969

Albert Y. Garner, novel phosphonyl polymers, March 1964; flame retardant, Nov. 1976

Vicent A. Gill, quick disconnect valved coupling, Aug. 1960

Joseph Gilliard, car park, Nov. 1956

Meredith C. Gourdine, electrogasdynamic method and appar. for detecting the properties of particulate matter entrained in gas, June 1969

Bessie V. Griffin, portable receptacle support, April 1951

Clyde E. Gurley, automatic telephone alarm app., April 1970; programmable external dial operating device, April 1970

Lloyd A. Hall, antioxidant composition, Aug. 1956; antioxidant material and use of etc., Nov. 1956

Virginia E. Halkl, embroidered fruit bowl wall hanging and kit, April 1977

Solomon Harper, electrical hair-treating implement, Aug. 1930; thermostatic controlled hair curlers, Aug. 1953; thermostatic controlled fur, etc., June 1955

Lydis M. Holmes, knockdown wheeled toy, Nov. 1950

Harry C. Hopkins, hearing aid, Sept. 1977

Darnley E. Howard, Sr., optical apparatus, etc., Jan. 1939

Darnley M. Howard, Jr., method of making Radome, etc., June 1969

Wilson E. Hull, sublimation timing switch, Nov. 1966; mass release mechanism for satellites, Jan. 1969

James B. Huntley, emergency fire-escape mechanism, April 1975

Henry Jackson, method and composition for autocatalytically depositing copper, April 1969

Donald E. Jefferson, triggered exploding wire device, Nov. 1966

Thomas L. Jennings, dry scouring, March 1821

John Johnson, wrench, April 1922

Frederick M. Jones, method and means for air conditioning, Dec. 1954

Howard S. Jones, Jr., antenna testing shield, April 1962; waveguide components, July 1962; magnetomechanical, Aug. 1966; conformal edgeslot radiators, Sept. 1977

Hubert Julian, airplane safety appliance, May 1921

Kenneth C. Kelly, linearly polarized monopulse lobing antenna, etc., Nov. 1962

Lawrence R. Kelly, Jr., programmable external dial, April 1970

Lester A. Lee, Sr., carbon dioxide laser fuels, March 1977

Maurice W. Lee, Sr., aromatic pressure cooker and smoker, Sept. 1959

Beatrice Kenner, sanitary belt, May 1956

Herbert Leonard, Jr., production of hydroxylamine hydrochloride, Jan. 1964; high-impact polystyrene, June 1971

James E. Lewis, antenna feed for two coordinate tracking radars, June 1968

Emanuel L. Logan, Jr., door bar latch, July 1971

Hugh D. MacDonald, rocket catapult, June 1969

William L. Muckelroy, leadless microminiature inductance element with closed etc., Sept. 1972; ceramic inductor, May 1974

George W. Nauflette, process for the synthesis of 2-fluoro, 2, 2-dinitroethanol, March 1972

Clarence Nokes, venetian-blind restringer, June 1958; lawn mower, Feb. 1963

Charles A. Peterson, Jr., power-generating apparatus, July 1968

Alfred G.B. Prater, gravity escape means, Feb. 1973

Edwin R. Russel, prep. of tungsten hexafluoride, etc., Nov. 1976

Adolphus Samms, rocket engine pump feed system, Sept. 1961

Dewey S.C. Sanderson, urinalysis machine, July 1970

Ralph W. Sanderson, hydraulic shock absorber, Jan. 1968

Howard L. Scott, treating human, animal and syn. hair with a H_2O-proof composition, March 1971

Jonathan S. Smith II, transparent zirconia comp. and process, March 1969

Samuel C. Smith, hardness tester, May 1976

Osborne C. Stafford, microware phase-shift device, Aug. 1970

George B.D. Stephens, cigarette holder and ash tray, Sept. 1956

Rufus Stokes, exhaust purifier, April 1968

Charles W. Tate, flexible and transparent lubricant housing for univ. joint, Jan. 1969

Asa J. Taylor, machine for assembling and disassembling, June 1942; fluid joint, Jan. 1948

Moddie Taylor, prep. of anhydrous alkaline earth halides, Aug. 1957; prep. of anhydrous lithium salts, Aug. 1962

Joseph Ausbon Thompson, Jr., foot warmer, May 1946; moist/dry lavatory and toilet tissue, Nov. 1975

Oliver L. Thompson, vehicle parking attachment, June 1925

Allen H. Turner, electrostatic paint system; Jan. 1962; electrostatic paint, Sept. 1962

M. Lucius Walker, Jr., laminar fluid nor element, Nov. 1969

Rufus J. Weaver, stairclimbing wheelchair, Nov. 1968

Charles E. Weir, high-pressure optical cell, Feb. 1963

Paul E. Williams, helicopter, Nov. 1962

Dudley G. Woodard, prep. of water-soluble acrylic copolymers for use, etc., April 1961

BIBLIOGRAPHY

The Negro in Our History, Carter G. Woodson, 1962, Washington, D.C.

Black Inventors of America, McKinley Burt, 1969

The Colored Inventors, Henry E. Baker, 1913

The Afro-American Inventor, C.R. Gibbs, 1975

Black Pioneers of Science and Invention, Louis Haber, 1970

Eight Black American Inventors, Robert C. Hayden, 1972

SUGGESTED READING

Virginia Hamilton, WED Dubois, A Biography, Thomas Y. Corwell, New York

Julius Hester, To Be a Slave, Scholaster Books, New York

Robet Lipstye, Free to Be Muhammad Ali, Harper & Row, New York

Linda Lowery, Martin Luther King Day, Carol Rhoda Books, Minneapolis, MN

Ann McGovern, Wanted Dead or Alive, The Story of Harriet Tubman, Scholaster Books, New York

Lillie Patterson, Frederick Douglass, 1. Freedom Fighter , Garrard Publishing Company, Champaign, Ill. 2. Martin Luther King, Jr., Man of Peace, Garrard Publishing, Champaign, Ill.

Levone Bennett, Jr., Pioneers in protest, Johnson Publishing Company, Chicago.

Margaret Boone-Jones, Martin Luther Kings, Jr., Childrens Press Chicago

Dorothy Chaplik, Up with Hope, A Biography of Jesse Jaackson, Dilion Press, Inc., Minneapolis, MN

Magaret C. Clark, Benjamin Banneker, Astronomer and Scientist, Garrard Publishing Company, Champaign, Ill.

Lincoln Collier, and Christopher Collier, Jump Ship to Freedom, Deli Yearling, New York

Eloise Greenfield, Mary McCleod Bethune, Thomas Y. Crowel, New York

Louis Haber, Black Pioneers of Science and Invention, Harcourt, New York

Laurene Santrey, Young Frederick Douglass, Fight for Freedom, Troll Associates

Conrad R. Stein, The Story of the Montgomery Bus Boycott, Childrens Press, Chicago–The Story of the Underground Railroad, Childrens Press, Chicago

Dorothy S. Strickland, Listen Children, Bantam, New York

INDEX